One-Minute
MORNING
DEVOTIONS

Marie D. Jones

Publications International, Ltd.

Marie D. Jones is an ordained minister and a contributing author of numerous books, including *Sisters, Mother, Grandmother, Friends, Graduation, Wedding,* and *A Mother's Daily Prayer Book.* She is a widely published writer and can be reached through her Web site, www.mariedjones.com.

Additional original quotations provided by: Elaine Wright Colvin, Lain Chroust Ehmann, Jennifer John Ouellette, Ellen F. Pill, and Donna Shryer.

CONTENTS

IT ONLY TAKES A MINUTE...

*E*ven just a moment spent in devotional prayer can lead to a lifetime filled with blessings. Praising God, telling him how your day went, and asking for his help and wisdom is what connects you to his loving and infinite presence, just as time spent thinking about God's will and word serves to comfort and heal you. Talking to God can be part of your daily routine; after all, your message to God doesn't have to be long and wordy.

The prayers, thoughts, and Bible verses in *One-Minute Morning Devotions* are intended to help you begin each day with a special moment of grace. By taking a minute or two to focus on turning inward, you'll find that God is, and always has been, waiting to help you. He wants to aid his children and answer their prayers. Whether you are asking for physical healing or peace within your home and heart, ruminating on emotional strength or a renewal of faith, or seeking a deeper understanding of God's will, he not only listens, but he also responds with wisdom, guidance, and comfort.

Spend a contemplative moment this morning with *One-Minute Morning Devotions.* No doubt you will soon find your life changing. Blessings will begin to appear, and miracles suddenly occur—though all were simply waiting for you to slow down long enough for them to find you. In the quiet solitude of devotional prayer, you are given the chance to be heard by a power far greater than yourself; a power that can lift you up when you are lonely, lost, and afraid; a power that blesses a grateful heart and fulfills a joyful spirit.

It only takes a minute to talk to God. The result is an eternity of knowing you are loved and cared for in return.

Rejoice always, pray without ceasing, give thanks in all circumstances; for this is the will of God in Christ Jesus for you.
—1 Thessalonians 5:16–18

Joy and the Blessings of Love

RENEWED AND REFRESHED

As I rise to face this miracle of a new day, I give praise to you, God, for the joy of renewal with which you fill my spirit. Each morning, I feel more energetic, healthier, and more able to face life with a smile on my face and a joyful expectancy in my heart. I can feel the sun on my skin, and I know that it is your light, your warmth, washing over me, letting me know that I can and will be healthy and happy. I am alive, and my body and mind are both becoming stronger and more resilient with each passing day. For that I am so thankful.

Health and cheerfulness mutually beget each other.
—Joseph Addison

CELEBRATION

The steadfast love of the Lord never ceases,
his mercies never come to an end; they are new
every morning; great is your faithfulness.
—Lamentations 3:22–23

I love being alive, God!
Thank you for each day of life you
have given me. I am especially grateful
for today, for the moments it contains—
opportunities for me to enjoy blessings of
all kinds. There are many people, places,
and experiences yet to come my way, and
I live in anticipation of these joys and
wonders. I begin celebrating life today
as I live in full awareness of this
priceless gift from your hand.

LOVE ABOVE ALL ELSE

It bears all things, believes all things, hopes all things, endures all things. Love never ends.

—1 Corinthians 13:7–8

God, you have given me the gift of love: love of you, love of self, and love of others. And this day I go forward with a heart overflowing with the newfound ability to love as I never had before. I have seen the blessings that come from simply reaching out in love, and I've been touched by your own amazing grace. My gift to you in return is to love who I can, when I can. I will try to love in any way I can, large or small, for no love is insignificant. Love cannot be measured. Love never ends.

Spreading the Love

*G*od, thank you for the special people who over the years have been just like family to me. I love to think of the times we've spent together, of the way they've influenced my life for the better, and of their abiding love and care for me. There have been times when they've seemed even more like family to me than anyone else. Please bless these dear members of my extended family, and keep them always in your care.

May God bless me and the family I've made.

DANCE OF PARENTS

*I*t's not polite to boast, but to you, knower of innermost thoughts, I whoop and holler in delight: I love being a parent! And I am sometimes the best parent around. My children are the finest.

Despite tiredness and worry, I have moments of sheer, cartwheeling, rainbow-dancing joy. I hope there are times when you say that of me. Maybe today you will, as I join my kids to play in the leaves, make snow angels, picnic, dance, or share pizza in celebration of just being together.

Take our hands and jump with us for joy!

All I don't know, Lord, is most apparent when children are around. Their curiosity is insatiable. I'm grateful I don't need all the answers, just a willingness to consider the questions and honor the questioners. Knock, seek, and ask are imperative verbs implying your blessing on our quests.

LAUGHTER AS MEDICINE

A glad heart makes a cheerful countenance....
A cheerful heart is a good medicine.
—Proverbs 15:13; 17:22

God, grant me the ability to laugh today, if not audibly, then in my heart. Help me to lighten up and find some relief in humor when things get too intense. Show me how to be sensitive to others and to gently lead them in the direction of a smile. Come, cheer my heart right now with your witty perspective on my life. Indeed, I can't add an inch to my height or a minute to my existence by worrying, no matter how hard I grit my teeth and clench my fists. God, I'm chuckling now, and I'm ready to face my world.

Of all days, the day on which one has not laughed is the one most surely wasted.
—Sébastien-Roch Nicolas De Chamfort

Teamwork

For mortals it is impossible,
but for God all things are possible.
—Matthew 19:26

We did it, God! You and me together!
We overcame the darkness of my challenging situation,
and now I arise to a new day of love and joy and peace in
my heart. I could not have fought this battle alone.
It was taking me to a dark place, and you stepped in
and took me by the hand, and we walked together into
the light. With you, all things are possible, and now
I am ready to leap out of bed and face my life with a new
perspective and a joy I've not felt in a long, long time.
We did it, God! You and me together!

My Family, My Joy

*N*o matter what each new day brings, I pray my family finds joy, health, and happiness. No matter what may come our way, I pray my family faces each challenge with courage, wisdom, and the knowledge that love is more powerful than fear. No matter what conflicts we may run into today, I pray my family will always remember that love is all that matters in the end and that our bond is stronger than any obstacle we may face, together or alone. May we always find joy, hope, and blessings in the miracle that is our family.

Instead of feeling overwrought with demands to the point of being overwhelmed, feel the overflowing joy that comes from daily life in the midst of a hustling, bustling family. The two halves make one marvelous whole of God's balance.

THE LOVE THAT NEVER FAILS

*I will sing of our steadfast love, O Lord, forever;
with my mouth I will proclaim your
faithfulness to all generations.*
—Psalm 89:1

This new morning offers me a fresh opportunity to
count my blessings and remind myself that I am always loved
and supported. No matter how dark the night before may
have been, your steadfast love emboldens me with courage
and fearlessness to face the day with a joyful heart.
Knowing you will never fail me, I am able to go forward
and spread that same love to others, sharing with them
the joy of just being alive and loved by a power far
greater than we could ever comprehend.

LITTLE BLESSINGS

I never used to find joy in life's day-to-day stuff, like getting everyone ready for work and school and walking to get the mail. But now each day is a prayer of praise and thanksgiving to you, God. Thank you for allowing me this chance to experience the tiniest of miracles that occur moment to moment, as well as those big, bold joys that come around every once in a while. I look at each second I am alive as a reason to be happy. What joy there is to be found in the little blessings, the simple things! Thank you, God, for showing me the light.

Happy is the person who knows that life's greatest treasures are often buried deep within the simplest things, waiting to be discovered by those who are paying attention.

WHAT LOVE CAN DO

*L*ord, I am amazed each and every day by the power of love to heal and transform me. I also find myself amazed by this great world around me. I pray you will always keep my eyes and my heart focused on this great gift, the astounding ability to love and be loved. Let each new day be a chance to love a little more, give a little more, share a little more, and live a little more. Let me be a vessel through which love flows ever outward, touching everyone the way your love has touched me.

At the touch of love, everyone becomes a poet.
—Plato

COMING UP ROSES

**Did I not tell you that if you believed,
you would see the glory of God?**
—John 11:40

What joy greets me as I rise this morning? What love awaits me to give and share? My faith has made me whole again, and your love has begun to heal the wounds I never thought would heal. Everything is coming up roses today, and though I know that each new day may bring more troubles to deal with, for now I am leaping with joy as my heart is given wings. I am happy in this moment, Lord, and that is more than I had ever dreamed possible during my darkest hours. Thank you.

Life's New Beginnings

MESSAGE OF GIGGLES

Bless the children, God of little ones,
with their giggles and wide-eyed awe, their awakening
assumption that today will be chock-full of surprises,
learning, and love. Neither missing nor wasting a minute,
they take nothing for granted, a message that blesses us.
We will go and do likewise.

Bless this little one of so few days.
May he be prosperous in all his ways.
Healthy in body and mind, growing strong and kind.
Bless this little one through all his days.
Hush, my dear, lie still and slumber,
Holy angels guard thy bed!
Heavenly blessings without number
Gently falling on thy head.
—Isaac Watts, *A Cradle Hymn*

New DIRECTION

Life is full of trade-offs, Lord, and I need
to make one. I want to venture off the fast track where
I'm losing more than I am gaining. Guide my search for a job
where I can have both a life and a living. Restore my balance;
not the checkbook kind, for it will change when I do.
Your balance is not found running in a circle, but along a
beckoning path where just enough is more than sufficient;
where money comes second to family, community, and self;
where success takes on new meaning; and where,
in giving my faith to you, I gain wealth beyond belief.

Blessed is he who has found his work;
let him ask no other blessedness. He has a work,
a life-purpose; he has found it and will follow it.
—Thomas Carlyle

A NEW BEGINNING

*W*hat a blessing to have a second chance!
Grant me the wisdom to use this opportunity wisely.
And save me from the fear that I'll fall into the same traps
as last time. I may have made mistakes in the past, but I'm
determined to learn from them and grow because of them.
This is a brand-new day, a whole new beginning, and I'm
lucky to be able to face it anew. I'm going to give it a go.
Thank you, Lord!

From each of life's misfortunes, large or small, comes a new
beginning, an opportunity to renew your faith in the future.
As you go about your day, let happiness land where it will,
in its own time and place.

THINGS TO DO LIST

Those who wait for the Lord shall renew their strength, they shall mount up with wings like eagles, they shall run and not be weary, they shall walk and not faint.

—Isaiah 40:31

I have to admit it: I'm not a young pup anymore. As time goes on, I find it harder and harder to get out the door and do all of the things I've always wanted. I don't want to leave my Things I'm Going to Do list with so many items unchecked. Lord, please help me conquer my list by giving me the strength and vitality to discover new adventures, meet new people, and learn new hobbies. After all—getting older doesn't mean I have to quit having fun, right? I pray that you will guide my way in this new era of adventure.

LƐARNING TO LOVƐ AGAIN

*G*od, teach me to love anew. I have been hurt and
want to believe that love can find me,
if only I open my heart to it. Help me to see
the light at the end of the long, dark tunnel
of my suffering and to know that I am worthy of having
the kind of love that is pure and true. Help me to be
strong within myself, love myself, and always know that
with the coming of each new morning is a fresh
opportunity to find the love I seek.

Love comforteth like sunshine after rain.
—William Shakespeare

STARTING A NEW CAREER

*L*ord, it's been a long time since I've been
in the working world, and I am anxious and afraid.
I look to you for the strength and courage I need to take
on this new chapter in my life, and I ask for your help in
making the best decisions as I go about my first day back
in the workforce. With you, Lord, I can overcome any
challenge or obstacle that comes my way. This new beginning
you have given me is exciting and scary, but I am so grateful
for the chance to work again. With you as my colleague,
it will be a great first day on the job.

Be willing to be a beginner every single morning.
—Meister Eckhart

FOR A HAPPY RETIREMENT

For everything there is a season,
and a time for every matter under heaven ...
—Ecclesiastes 3:1

I woke up today with nothing to do and, for the first time in a long while, with no place I had to be. Retirement is a very scary thing. I know it is up to me to make the best of this extra time, to live my dreams and do whatever I please, but I feel as though I have no purpose. Help me, Lord, to find the next step along my life path. I don't have to save the world or climb a mountain or cure a disease—though there are plenty of those in need whom I could help. Just help me learn how to fill each blessed hour with joy, enthusiasm, and a sense that I am truly worthy of the freedom to spend my time doing exactly what makes me happy.

Picking up the Pieces

*The stone that the builders rejected has become
the cornerstone; this was the Lord's doing,
and it is amazing in our eyes.*

—Matthew 21:42

The turmoil I am experiencing from losing my job has
left me feeling so lost, alone, and unworthy. I feel as though I
have failed so many people, especially my family, and I
cannot do anything right. I ask for strength today as
I pick up the pieces and try to make something better of
my life. My job status may have fallen, but my faith in you
never wavers, and I know that with your love and guidance,
Lord, I can and will begin again. And I can and will always
remember that in your eyes I am worthy.

SURVIVING HEARTBREAK

The spirit of the Lord God is upon me,
because the Lord has anointed me;
he has sent me to bring good news to the oppressed,
to bind up the broken-hearted . . .

—Isaiah 61:1

As this love relationship comes to an end, my heart grieves for my loss. There are mornings when I awaken and feel like I don't know how to get through the day. But your love reminds me that I am still alive and worthy of a new life. One day, I know that I will find a new love, someone who will make my heart feel light. With your strength to carry me through this day, I know I can manage the pain and see the possibilities that are waiting just around the corner.

A NEW FAMILY

*G*od, you have blessed me with the joy of a new child and the beginnings of a growing family. I am afraid and excited, anxious yet overjoyed. I am worried but welcoming of this miraculous new life I have brought into the world. I pray for the courage, faith, and fortitude to be the best parent I can be, now and always. I know it won't all be giggles and smiles, but it will all be amazing, wonderful, and worth every second. Thank you for giving me this gift of life and for trusting this child to my care.

Caring for a baby is like opening a treasure chest full of shiny new experiences and precious, priceless moments.

Home is Where the Heart is

*For where your treasure is,
there your heart will be also.*

—Matthew 6:21

We are leaving our old home behind and moving into a new home in a whole new neighborhood. My heart is having a hard time letting go of this old house and all the warm and wonderful memories we made here. But help me to understand, Lord, that home is really where my heart is and that my memories will go with me wherever I go. After all, a home is more than just walls, floors, and rooms. May your abiding love always remind me that no matter where I wake up tomorrow morning, I will truly be at home.

A Better World

OPPORTUNITIES

And God is able to provide you with every
blessing in abundance, so that by always having
enough of everything, you may share abundantly
in every good work.
—2 Corinthians 9:8

Each day as I look about me,
I discover unlimited opportunities.
Every person I meet is an opportunity to uncover
a biography, see through different eyes, find a friend.
Each place I go is an opportunity to
try a new route, enjoy the scenery along the way,
explore my surroundings, create an adventure.
Each sunrise, flower, book, meal, walk,
conversation—each encounter in life—
is an opportunity to seize the day.
God, let my life be lived in praise to you as
I take hold of the opportunities you give me.

MINDING OUR MANNERS

*I*t's hard to be pleasant on these rude,
road-raging days. Everyone's too immersed in their
own concerns to be mannerly or kind. Encourage me
to get in the first "please," "thanks," and "excuse me";
remind me to take turns on the road, in the store, at work.
Maybe good manners will be as contagious as rude ones.
May I, with your guidance, be first to pass them on.

*Life is not so short that there is always
time enough for courtesy.*
—Ralph Waldo Emerson

Spreading Our Light

No one after lighting a lamp puts it under
the bushel basket, but on the lampstand,
and it gives light to all in the house.

—Matthew 5:15

We have each been given our own unique talents and
gifts to share with the world. Lord, help me to recognize
these gifts and to share them with those around me. But
even more importantly, help me teach others to share their
gifts and shine their own lights. We are all miracles of your
creation, and nothing would make me happier today than to
express who I am by shining my light and seeing others do
the same. Imagine what the world would be like: more
happiness, fulfillment, joy, and an end to darkness forever.

ROOM FOR ONE MORE

Finally, all of you, have unity of spirit, sympathy, love for one another, a tender heart, and a humble mind.

—1 Peter 3:8

*I*f we are to believe the headlines, opposites don't attract nearly as often as they repel. Pick a race, color, creed, or lifestyle, and we'll find something to fight about. Deliver us from stereotypes, and inspire us to spot value in everyone we meet. As we dodge the curse of bigotry and hatred, we are relieved to find there is room for all of us beneath your wings. Bless our diversity; may it flourish.

You have said: We are all one. So when I am tempted to separate, alienate, or exasperate my sisters and brothers, remind me: We are all one.

$\mathcal{E}$XPANDING OUR VISION

$\mathcal{I}$ pray this day that every man, woman, and child may experience a greater, grander vision of what life could be. I pray that miracles both big and small occur in places far and wide and that we all come to a better understanding of just how this web of life connects us to one another. I pray for peace, love, and joy. I pray that those who suffer realize there is help in a power far greater than themselves, and the boundaries of what's possible go far beyond time and space.

Take time to reflect on the people and things around you. It is in these quiet moments that inspiration grows and we recognize the miracle of life.

V*ESSEL OF PEACE*

*G*od, fill me this morning with the light of your peace
that it may shine through me and touch everyone
I come in contact with today. Make me your instrument,
speaking and working through me, to spread love and
promote a greater understanding of tolerance and justice.
Help me to first find my steadfast peace within and then
go forward and share it with others, helping them
to discover their own inner serenity.

*Lord, make me an instrument of your peace,
where there is hatred, let me sow love;
where there is injury, pardon;
where there is doubt, faith . . .*
—St. Francis of Assisi

CHOICES

But I say to you that listen, Love your enemies,
do good to those who hate you, bless those who
curse you, pray for those who abuse you.
—Luke 6:27–28

My prayer today is simple. I pray that each and every choice I make be made with an open heart, a loving spirit, and a mind that sees both sides of the equation. There is enough violence and anger in this world; I ask you, God, to help me make the choices today that will best serve the good of all. Let me add light to the world with my actions, not darkness. Let each decision I make move me, and everyone around me, into a higher place of being.

THE TOUGH STUFF

*Oh Lord, when I see terrible, fearful events—
explosions destroying whole buildings, droughts turning
crops to dust, storms devastating all in their path—then
I turn to you. And you are always here, listening, caring,
and waiting for all of us to reach out to you. Amen.*

There are many events in our lives over which we have no
control. However, we do have a choice either to endure trying
times and press on or to give up. The secret of survival, whether
or not we question God's presence or his ability to help us, is
remembering that our hope is in the fairness, goodness, and
justice of God. When we put our trust in the character of a
God who cannot fail us, we will remain faithful. Our trust and
faithfulness produce the endurance that sees us through the
"tough stuff" we all face in this life.

WHAT IF?

No good tree bears bad fruit,
nor again does a bad tree bear good fruit;
for each tree is known by its own fruit.

—Luke 6:43–44

hat if we could all bear good fruit? As I arise,
I ask myself that question. Today I will face a whole
new opportunity to bear good fruit and to see the result
in my world. I pray that others also may realize that it is
the quality of their fruit that shapes the quality of their lives,
and that we can all make the world a much better place
if we are aware of that. Today I will try to bear the best
fruit I can, with the hope that it will ripen and give seed
to even better fruit tomorrow.

THE GREATER GOOD

If I have all faith, so as to remove mountains,
but do not have love, I am nothing. If I give away
all my possessions . . . so that I may boast,
but do not have love, I gain nothing.

—1 Corinthians 13:2-3

I pray that today I can do something to contribute
to the greater good. Whether it is a big display of charity or
a small and random act of kindness, I pray to do whatever
I can to strengthen my strand in the web of life. May my
words come out kind and loving, and may my actions be
for the greater good. I know I am not perfect, but I pray
I can reach a little higher today to be a better person and
make the world just a little bit nicer in some way.

STAND FOR TRUTH

Then Jesus said . . . "If you continue in my word,
you are truly my disciples; and you will know
the truth, and the truth will make you free."
—John 8:31-32

God, I ask this morning for the courage and faith to speak from truth today. Let no outside influence shape my perception, but instead help me to keep focused on what is right and just and true—even if others tell me I am wrong. I ask for support in standing for truth. Perhaps, in doing so, others will look to me as a model for courage, and they will try to behave in kind. Like dominoes, let us all affect one another positively.

Healing the Mind, Body, and Spirit

A NEW DAY

Everything looks much
brighter than it did before.
My prayer for strength has
been answered.
My cries for help have been heard.
My pleas for mercy flew directly
to your throne.
Now I'm ready to help
my neighbor, Lord.
Let me not delay.

*Between the humble and contrite heart and the majesty of
heaven there are no barriers; the only password is prayer.*
—Hosea Ballou

IN SICKNESS AND IN HEALTH

*L*ord, keep me in your heart this morning.
My marriage is suffering from all sorts of ills, and I wonder
if our love can survive. We stood before you on our wedding
day and promised to stand by one another in sickness and
in health, but sometimes it seems as though the tough
times are breaking us apart. We are not handling these
difficulties well, and we ask for your help. Send some
healing our way so we can weather the bad times just
as we celebrate the good times—as a team who has
vowed to love each other until death do us part.

Marriage is not a guarantee of "happily ever after", but a
promise of moving through life together "come what may."

POOR IN SPIRIT

The poor shall eat and be satisfied;
those who seek him shall praise the Lord.
—Psalm 22:26

Lord, you are my food, my sustenance, my healing.
My spirit has been made weak and small because of my
fears and challenges, but each morning you give me the
ingredients I need to become just a little bit stronger.
Even if it is only one day at a time, with your love,
guidance, and healing power, I know I can indeed get
through these next 24 hours and that it will get easier
and easier as the days go by. I thank you, God,
for making my spirit stronger.

How do I cope?

He has sent me to proclaim release to the captives,
and recovery of sight to the blind,
to let the oppressed go free.

—Luke 4:18

The news of my illness has been hard to take,
but I lift up my eyes and my heart to you, God, to forever
remind me of your mercy and to soothe me with the healing
balm of your love. If I remain centered in the grace of your
will for me, I know I can find the strength inside to live
and to experience healing that my doctors would call
miraculous. My faith is strong, and I know this experience
will only serve to make it stronger. In you, God, let me
find wholeness and freedom from this disease.

Silver Linings

**Weeping may linger for the night,
but joy comes with the morning.**

—Psalm 30:5

*J*ust as each cloud is lined with silver, so, too, is each
painful experience lined with the miracle of
lessons learned and wisdom gained. God never
takes something from us without giving us
something else in return.

God, hear my prayer. Bless me with patience and
a steadfast heart to help me get through such emotionally
trying times. Heal the wounds of my heart and soul with
the soothing balm of your comforting presence, that
I may be able to love and live again. Amen.

WHERE IS THE JOY?

Blessed are you who are hungry now,
for you will be filled. Blessed are you who
weep now, for you will laugh.

—Luke 6:21

Things around the office here have been rough, and I often find myself waking up each morning dreading the workday ahead of me. I used to be happy and smiling, but now I feel like I've lost my love of life. I ask for your healing spirit to come upon me and fill me with a new appreciation for what I am and what I have. Help me to recover my childlike sense of wonder and my ability to find joy in both the big and the small things I experience each day. Thank you, God, for giving me a healing light for my dark and shadowed spirit.

FIRST STEPS

The Lord will guide you continually,
and satisfy your needs in parched places,
and make your bones strong...
—Isaiah 58:11

I have been unable to do much since my injury,
and my body only mirrors my broken spirit.
God, I ask of you this day to give me the strength to get up
and take those first steps toward healing. It may be hard,
but I know that with the power of your love and mercy,
I can do anything I set my mind to.

THERE SHALL BE LAUGHTER

A cheerful heart has a continual feast.
—Proverbs 15:15

*M*y Creator, I know in my heart these tears will
one day give way again to joy, yet for now I know only pain.
Help me to find the courage to let these tears flow, to feel
the loss and heartbreak, so that I may come out whole and
cleansed again. For on the other side of my sorrow
I know life waits for me. I want to laugh again.

It's often easy to get mired in a spiral of downward thinking.
When this happens, try literally counting your blessings.
For instance, think about the people who energize you with
their humor, and be grateful for their presence in your life!

OF ANXIOUS MIND

*I called to the Lord out of my distress,
and he answered me...*

—Jonah 2:2

God, it sometimes seems as though I cannot stop
worrying about my children, my spouse,
my career, and my finances. There is always something
plaguing my mind and stealing peace from my heart.
I ask for your guidance and strength, that I may
turn over my worries to you and go on living my life
as best I can, knowing that if I am called upon to face
any challenge, you will be right there beside me.
Calm my anxious mind and rest my worries, God,
so that I can make this life you gave me the happy,
joyous experience I know you meant it to be.

A PARENT'S LAMENT

*When Jesus saw this, he . . . said to them, "Let the little
children come to me; do not stop them; for it is to such
as these that the kingdom of God belongs."*
—Mark 10:14

God, help me heal the rift between my child
and me. It is hard being a parent, and I
need all the help I can get. My over-worrying and
my wanting to be in control got the best of me.
I often react in ways that are not positive and
constructive, and I need your grace and wisdom
to find just the right words to say and actions to take
to be the best parent I can be. Help me each morning
to be a stronger, more secure, and more loving
parent than I was the day before.

Courageous Faith: Letting Go and Letting God

SURPRISING STRENGTH

I can do all things through him who strengthens me.
—Philippians 4:13

As we learn to trust you, God, we discover
your strengthening presence in various places and people.
Wherever we encounter shelter, comfort, rest, and peace,
we are bound to hear your voice welcoming us.
And in whomever we find truth, love, gentleness, and
humility, we are certain to hear your heartbeat,
assuring us that you will always be near.

FRIGHTENING DIAGNOSIS

O Lord, be gracious to us; we wait for you.
Be our arm every morning,
our salvation in the time of trouble.

—Isaiah 33:2

I don't think I've ever been more scared than when my doctor told me about my condition. If I've ever needed your help to get out of this bed and get on with my day, now is the time. I don't know why this is happening to me or what the ultimate outcome will be, but I am turning it all over to you. I know you will only give me what I can handle, and I trust that there is a higher reason behind this challenge I am about to face.

STANDING TALL

*All the trees of the field shall know
that I am the Lord. I bring low the high tree,
I make high the low tree...*

—Ezekiel 17:24

God, I feel small and tired today as I start my day.
Things have been tough in my life lately,
and my faith is being tested moment by moment.
I know that there is a mighty courage within me,
and I ask you now to help me remember that I am like
the tree that stands tall, roots firmly planted,
bending with the wind, not against it. With you as my roots,
I will never break, no matter how strong the wind.
Thank you, God, for faith renewed.

RIGHT NOW

*L*et me do what lies clearly at hand this very minute.
Grant me the insight to see that too much planning for the
future removes me from the present moment.
This is the only existence, the only calling I have been
given—to do what is necessary right now.
Nothing more, nothing less.
Thus, may I use this next moment wisely.

God, grant me the insight to see the positive purposes
you have for me in each day, and fill me with the peace
that comes from living by that insight.

LEARNING TO DETACH

Let your eyes look directly forwards,
and your gaze be straight before you.
—Proverbs 4:25

There is someone I love, God, who has an addiction, and I know I must learn to detach from the problem in order to really help the person. But it is so hard to let go of control, for fear and worry that they will use again and sink deeper into despair. If I can let go and surrender this problem to you, only then will this person have a chance to truly walk a path toward wholeness and healing. I cannot do it for them; I must walk my own path and focus on my own healing. Give me the courage, God, to detach in a loving and supportive way.

FROM DOUBT, FAITH

*L*ord, I know I can be a real doubting Thomas at
times, and that my doubts get me into places where nothing
in my life seems to fit. This morning I ask that you give me a
bold and courageous fire of faith to fuel me through my day,
reminding me that by surrendering my will to you,
I will always be rewarded with blessings. I may not see those
blessings today, but I have faith they are unfolding, even
as my doubt threatens to blind me to them.

If you would be a real seeker after truth,
it is necessary that at least once in your life you doubt,
as far as possible, all things.
—René Descartes

Moving on with Life

Blessed be God,
because he has not rejected my prayer
or removed his steadfast love from me.
—Psalm 66:20

Lord, when my loved one died I thought I could
never go on, but with each new morning I find that by
turning to you and giving control of my life to you, I am
renewed with the strength I need to get by. I know the path
ahead is filled with suffering, loss, grief, and anguish, but I
am moving on with the help of your grace and love.
And in those moments when all is dark and bleak,
I give my burdens up to you, knowing you will always
receive them from me and lighten my load.

ALL FOR THE BEST

God, I often push and push toward a certain goal,
only to have my dreams fall flat. I work hard,
but sometimes things just don't seem to work out.
Today I will try to surrender my dreams to you and know
that whatever the outcome, it will be for my highest
and best good. It is hard to give up control, but being
controlling hasn't gotten me very far, has it? Help me
to let go of my attachments, my insistence on having
things my way, and instead let things happen your way...
the way they were meant to happen.

*If we do not find anything pleasant,
at least we will find something new.*
—Voltaire

GIVING UP CONTROL

**So do not worry about tomorrow,
for tomorrow will bring worries of its own.
Today's trouble is enough for today.**
—Matthew 6:34

I don't know how to handle this illness that has taken over my body. I am so tired and down all the time, even after a good night's sleep. My way is simply not working toward healing, and I need to change my approach. Instead, I am putting you in charge of my body, my energy, and my healing. In return, I promise to have faith, keep my wits about me, and continue to give up control when I find I am holding on too hard to what is just not working.

TODAY FIRST

*I*n this time of change, help me to be patient, God.
Let me not run ahead of you and your plans.
Give me courage to do only what is before me and to keep
my focus on my responsibilities. I am tempted to daydream
about tomorrow; however, the future is in your hands.
Thus, may I be close to you in all my thoughts and
accomplish the task before me today.

Spirit of God, keep teaching me the ways of change and
growth. Like the wind, you cannot be tracked or traced.
The breezes blow where they will, silently, invisibly, with great
power—just as you are working in lives even now. Let me know
your call as you move in me! Whisk through all the windows of
my soul and the dark corners of my heart.

Guidance and Wisdom

WHY AM I HERE?

*L*ord, I know that you gave me the precious gift of life
for a reason, and on this bright new day, I ask for your
guidance in directing me to the people, places, and situations
that will bring out the talents and skills locked within me.
I long to be of service and to do good things—*great* things—
in the world, but I do not know how or where to begin.
I thank you for this gift of life, and now I want to give of
myself to others. Help me find the best way to do that.

Remember you are the promise and the hope of the future.
Remember you are the very essence of life.
Remember you were born for a purpose.

CULTIVATE YOUR FAITH

The apostles said to the Lord,
"Increase our faith!" The Lord replied,
"If you had faith the size of a mustard seed,
you could say to this mulberry tree, 'Be uprooted
and planted in the sea,' and it would obey you."
—Luke 17:5–6

Faith is the touchstone of our relationship with God.
It is a great and glorious experience when it is sufficient and
can seem like our undoing when it is not.

With practice, faith is as simple as taking a breath.
Today, believe God for one small thing—it will be
the beginning of your walk with faith.

Lord, teach me to walk with faith,
whether with baby steps or giant strides.

TURNING PAIN INTO LAUGHTER

Rejoice in hope, be patient in suffering,
persevere in prayer.
—Romans 12:12

Your soul can dance though pain is here.
Call healing music to your ear.
Spot emotion's fickle turning,
Leap in love,
Stretch hopes,
Master fear's deep strains.
Dare to dance both health and pain.
However clumsy, long, or fleeting,
We dance life well if grace is leading.

Fork in the Road

Commit your cause to the Lord; let him deliver—
let him rescue the one in whom he delights!
—Psalm 22:8

have a big decision to make today, God,
and I ask your guidance and wisdom as I come upon this
fork in the road of my life. As I ask myself which path to
take, let me hear the whisperings of divine direction urging
me to step upon the one path that will truly lead me to my
best good. Let not my ego nor petty fears and doubts cloud
my choice, for it is your path I wish to walk, God, the one
you have chosen for me. Let your will be done. Amen.

HOW DO I HANDLE THIS?

*G*od, I am facing a tough day ahead, for I have unwittingly hurt loved ones and caused them great offense. Help me choose just the right things to say and do in order to set this situation right again and heal our relationship. I do not know how to handle such a challenge on my own, but with your wisdom and guidance, I know I will be able to bring light into a dark place and rectify the wrong I have done.

When honesty is tempered with tact,
a relationship built on trust is born.

THE MEANING OF MY LIFE

Those who find their life will lose it,
and those who lose their life for my sake will find it.
—Matthew 10:39

Sometimes when I am caught up in the craziness
of my day, I forget why I am here, and what your divine plan
is for me. I ask that you gently remind me to slow down
every now and then and listen for guidance, the inner call
of your spirit, and for the divine spark of wisdom deep
within. Only then will I be able to rise above the busyness
of everyday life and remember just how much of a miracle
you gave me when you gave me this life.

ONLY HUMAN

And forgive us our debts,
as we also have forgiven our debtors.
—Matthew 6:12

God, I know that I am only human, and that means
I make mistakes and say the wrong things
quite often. But you created me in your image,
and I ask you to help guide me toward living a more
divinely inspired life. Let me be the best human I can be,
even as I strive toward being more like you. And if and
when my humanity does not serve others, or myself,
give me a sign, and I will readily work to correct my ways.
So let it be done.

A LITTLE LOST TODAY

**Your word is a lamp to my feet
and a light to my path.**
—Psalm 119:105

*L*ord, as I wake up this morning, I am feeling a little lost and uncertain. I am not sure of what I should do, how best to spend my time and efforts today. I am grateful for your guidance and that you've given me the opportunity to spend a few quiet moments in prayer listening for your voice. Only when I hear you can I truly know that I am right where I should be, doing exactly what I must. In you, God, I am always home and never alone.

LEAPING

*S*ometimes leaping can be scary, Lord. You know, that little mental push into doing something I've never tried. I'm not entirely sure if I'll be successful, but if I don't try, I'll never know what amazing things I'm capable of. Help me realize if I make a mistake, it's okay. My mistakes—and the lessons I've learned by making them—have contributed to making me who I am. So today I'm going to just close my eyes, have faith in you and myself, and leap!

Faith is a true sign of bravery. It is looking forward to the future despite challenges and adversity; it is trusting in something that you can neither see nor touch yet know is always there guiding you along life's path.

WHERE IS THE LESSON?

For whatever was written in former days was written for our instruction, so that by steadfastness and by the encouragement of the scriptures we might have hope.
—Romans 15:4

I know that somewhere in this difficult situation there is a wonderful and empowering lesson for me to learn. But right now, God, I must admit that I am unable to see it, even after a good night's sleep. Bring me the inner guidance I seek, to help me understand and be able to move on from this challenge. I know the answers are there, waiting for me to hear them, so speak to me today, God. I am ready, and willing, to listen.

THE BLESSIN' IN THE LESSON

*T*each me, O Lord, to always find the blessin' in the lesson. For every challenge and obstacle I face, for every trial and tribulation that comes my way, let me remember to be grateful for the outcome, and for the wisdom and strength I have gleaned from it. Even in the most adverse of circumstances, when I cannot see the solution, help me find the light, the truth, and the gift that can bring me to a deeper level of joy and understanding. Let me always give thanks for my troubles, for in the end they bring out the best in me.

It is difficulties that show what men are.
—Epictetus

Praise and Gratitude

MORNING, GOD!

How good it is to sing praises to our God;
for he is gracious, and a song of praise is fitting.
—Psalm 147:1

*J*ust the fact that I am breathing as
I wake up this morning...
Just the fact that I can see the sun streaming
through my window...
Just the fact that I can hear the birds singing outside...
It all gives me reason to say thank you, God, for giving me
one more day to get things right. I am grateful to be alive,
despite the problems and challenges I face. I rise with
enthusiasm for a new and fresh opportunity to do things
differently today than I did yesterday.
Thank you, thank you, thank you!

Minor Miracles

*L*ord, I am grateful this new day for the little things: the warm sun on my face, the smell of fresh coffee brewing in the kitchen, the laughter of children, even the morning television show I watch as I prepare for a new day. I know I often thank you for the big things in my life, God, but I wanted to take the time today to thank you for the small stuff as well. After all, it is the small details that add richness and texture and depth to my life, making each moment a miracle to treasure.

We find great things are made of little things,
And little things go lessening till at last
Comes God behind them.
—Robert Browning

SUNRISE

Sing to the Lord with thanksgiving;
make melody to our God on the lyre. He covers
the heavens with clouds, prepares rain for the earth,
makes grass grow on the hills.

—Psalm 147:7–8

I marvel as I awaken each morning at the blessings you've bestowed upon me. Thanks be to you for another day filled with the possibilities of all good things. Your abundance fills my heart as I open my curtains and take in the view of the world you have created. From the gentle flowers that sway in the morning breeze, to the children happily running off to school, I am filled with gratitude for this bright new chance to show you my love, just as you never fail to show me yours.

TODAY: CAUSE FOR CELEBRATION

*W*ith boldness, wonder, and expectation,
I greet you this morning, God of sunrise. Gratefully,
I look back to all that was good yesterday and, in hope,
face forward, ready for today.

Good morning, God!
We greet you with our many morning faces:
We arise sometimes grumpy, sometimes smiling,
sometimes prepared, sometimes behind. But each day holds
the promise of a life knowing you are by our side.
Always may we turn to you first in our family prayer.
Bless us today.

MORNING

*G*od, it is always the right time to worship you,
but morning is best.
Praise for the dawning light that streams in
through the window.
Praise for the sounds of the birds as they flit
through the air.
Praise for the flowering plants—and even
those weeds growing by the house.
Most of all, praise for the breath that keeps
flowing in and out of my lungs.
Yes, this is the greatest item of praise:
that you alone are my life—all life itself.
Praise . . . for you.

How good it is, Almighty One, to bask in the warmth
of your love. To know nothing more than this:
receive your good gifts from above.

SUPERHERO

*N*o matter what challenges I face today, I know you will never fail me. No matter what trials may be waiting as I get out of bed and prepare for my day, I know you will be right there beside me, God, to offer me grace, wisdom, and understanding. I can always count on you to show me the best solutions to whatever problems I face. Thank you for being my superhero, ready to help me leap tall buildings in a single bound should I not be able to leap them by myself.

A mighty fortress is our God,
a bulwark never failing.
—Martin Luther

GRATEFUL FOR IT ALL

God, please forgive me if I sometimes forget to thank you for the bad things as well as the good. Sure, it's the blessings of abundant love and joy that fill my heart with gratitude, but I am also thankful for the rough spots in life that help me smooth my edges and learn the lessons I was put here on Earth to learn. Those moments may be very difficult at times and can fill my heart with fear, but I know in the end they are shaping and molding me into my best self. And for that, God, I am most grateful.

A grateful person knows that by giving thanks, they're given even more to be thankful for.

TELLING THE FAMILY TALE

*T*hank you for the gift of memory.
Playing "I remember" is such fun, especially sharing
it with grandchildren. Like relay runners, they are here
to pick up their part of our family tale.

Lord, you are the God who has set the foundations of the earth,
who blessed Abraham with offspring "as numerous as the stars
in heaven." You have blessed me, too, by giving me the treasure
of my heart: my family. I pour out my thanks for these gifts,
which are far above any riches the world can give.
How can I praise you enough?

Thou who has given so much to me,
give me one thing more: a grateful heart.
—George Herbert

SING OUT, HEART!

God, you have blessed me with so much to be grateful for today. I often wonder what I have done to be so deserving until I remember that we are all your beloved children and that we are all worthy. I have so much to do today, with work and family obligations, so I wanted to make sure I started my morning off by thanking you, God, for all you have done and all you continue to do for me and my loved ones. Your blessings make my heart sing out in joyful praise!

Gratitude is the memory of the heart.
—Jean Baptiste Massieu

THANKSGIVING

O come, let us sing to the Lord;
let us make a joyful noise to the rock of our salvation!
Let us come into his presence with thanksgiving;
let us make a joyful noise to him with songs of praise!
For the Lord is a great God,
and a great King above all gods.
In his hand are the depths of the earth;
the heights of the mountains are his also.

—Psalm 95:1–4

Heavenly Father, I never fail to come to you for
help and comfort in the dark times of my life, yet I don't
always remember you when my cup is overflowing.
Forgive me if I seem ungrateful and take your generosity for
granted. How can I forget all that you give me each day?
You bring beauty, peace, and love to my existence.
My heart overflows with thanksgiving.